GIRLWOOD

GIRLWOOD
Jennifer Still

Brick Books

Library and Archives Canada Cataloguing in Publication

Still, Jennifer, 1973-
    Girlwood / Jennifer Still.

Poems.
ISBN 978-1-926829-66-1

    I. Title.

PS8637.T54G57 2010   C811'.6   C2010-907672-9

Copyright © Jennifer Still, 2011

We acknowledge the Canada Council for the Arts, the Government of Canada through the Canada Book Fund, and the Ontario Arts Council for their support of our publishing program.

The cover photograph, "68 Girdwood Crescent, 1975," was taken by Jim Still.

The author photograph was taken by Jennifer Beaudry.

The book is set in Berkeley Oldstyle and Trajan.

Design and layout by Alan Siu.

Printed and bound by Sunville Printco Inc.

Brick Books
431 Boler Road, Box 20081
London, Ontario N6K 4G6

www.brickbooks.ca

*To the Girdwood girls;
and for Abby, for Joan.*

And we start, with a new and terrible energy, to write the poems of the imagined real place.

> Robert Kroetsch

Not fragments but metonymy. Duration. Language makes tracks.

> Lyn Hejinian

SKIPPING SONG

you are the other side of the tracks girl

the step around the crack or you'll break your mother's back girl

the itsy bitsy teeny weeny rack girl

the last to be picked for the team and the first to get to first base girl

you've got to color within the black lines girl

you've got your pennies lined up on the rail girl

you've got your boxcar vibe and your bangs combed high

and your hand held tight to the tremor girl—

TRACKS

SKIPPING SONG   9

TRACK 1   13

NEST   15

TRACK 2   29

SNAKESKIN   31

TRACK 3   49

THE HUMMINGBIRD
VIGNETTES   51

TRACK 4   81

MOTH   83

TRACK 5   99

LEAF   101

NOTES   115

ACKNOWLEDGEMENTS   117

TRACK 1

you could be   at every turn   the story of the girl
you were, there are things you shouldn't be seeing now from such
a comfortable seat, two feet above disaster Nike high-top wedged
in the rails, you learn to move swiftly from a stuck position, when
the penny trembles and you wear it, your fear of gym class, game
lines, the foul, the centre and especially the key, team dynamic
thunders by like the danger of a black van with velvet curtains,
and you wait for it, the worm body to drop, wet and knotted,
unknotted, snotty-nose dripping, the flinch right there at your
palm, avoid the gashes all the way to school   *don't look down* at the
bloated blue veins, the old soul backs of your hands smeared in
Cover Girl concealer, *to blend in   blend in* you safety-pin your
jeans on the outer seam all the way so they need coat-hanger
leverage, a starved stomach, to be tough so tough they are washed
with acid and stones, you can barely feel his hand in the matinee
darkness creeping your upper thigh, an itch you swat at   it
          it   it it you use ketchup to write *perv* on the sidewalk
and the flies the flies eat the word, a white squirm where eyes used
to be, the boys lay the cat back on the track and all it takes is speed
to blow dandelion to fur, wishes *your wishes* to scream, *learn the*

power of 9, said the palmist, *sign your name with the ifer*, the coarse
hair on his knuckles, your willingness to believe, fate is a husband
at eighteen a child at twenty *what education serves us if at all*, Sunday
morning Bible Leaders class, *Mom calls it Bible Eaters*, and the
growing hunger all those years for meaning, bus-kid lunch hours
Candace cat-squeezes the back of your neck so hard you choke on
your own skin, *don't   don't   tell* oh god, god is there in the
crossing gates lowering over you, red lamps tied to his ankles

      swinging   swinging   bells

NEST

these are my contents

Carolyn Forché

pendulum

somewhere

over the navel—

what is yes what is no what floats freely at your chest what in the middle of it all what hair in the locket what chain what silver clicks in your throat what stitch before your hands what small spotlight in the night what machine what file what bone on the tapping what beauty mark up the sleeve what pattern what knot what neckline what rope what cut what hand what creamy weave of vein what tree what branch what arc

in the new form

taking?

68 girdwood

panic on the crescent
something's coming

crescendo of steel
on steel, butter knives

sparking her high-heel staccato
pacing the blades the   *clickety-clack*

candy houses crack   *pink yellow blue*

new windows, doors
stucco, calcite bright

gather the shells

thin walls in thin dyes

in a warm basket

in a pendant light, rock her

back and back

to the chains, the chains of her

swag lamp swaying

night

freight
in the nail heads

a shunt
under

the eggshell sheen

count

the breaks the cars the creaks the stars the whistles the pennies the unlucky cows the shadows the stairs the switches the taps the witches the baths the serpents the eggs the silver clicks of her rings *timing*

forward, with a pin in her mouth
before the sulfur winds the yoke

to drain an egg

needle

down down

into the raw

insert

your breath, let it out

let out

the grief

in one long golden thread

sunset

spooned in the oval
mirror, my pink walls

swivel, dark
and darker

a tint in the paint, a split

what will we become?

hairbrush

bobby pins, our centre-parts
flicked, frosted, small wings
at our temples, nests
wound in our pulse, knots
stranded at our ends

safety

is the fencing it takes
to hold us back
from the pink flamingoes,
agitating sprinklers, neighbours
tsktsktsking at neighbours who don't
weed-bar their lawns, the amber
sirens, malathion trucks
dosing us just enough
to survive
the nuisances in the air

living room

crushed and crushed
the gold carpet takes
the logical formations
of sofa, TV trays, La-Z-Boy
in relation to chips & dips
coaster rings, empty

the room and you will find
the fixed position of our gaze
how far we were willing
to reach

built

with dandelions in Dixie cups, Cream of Wheat sputter, small lumps, bra bumps, egg cups, ivory lace, with the center shaped to what is not yet there *everything made for what is not yet there,* 70s couch autumns, golds we were lost in when it came to the family photo, floral upon floral, pear upon pear, our pearls our perms our brown velour our down, Love's Baby Soft, shouldered mists of rose, the simple need to sling ourselves completely, with wood dowel, bead, the small hammer of our chests, a love for general instructions, the art of decorative knotting, macramé, Jell-O moulds, kettle-wet windows, with loveseats, velvet flowers, paper tole forest scenes, seed filling our palms, fates sprouting mid-air, oscillating water, pendulum strokes, with foods that match the furniture, butterscotch, Jiffy Pop, flowered pots of KD, with wood-look products in vinyl, lampshades under plastic, things saved for saving's sake, with lint, *picking and picking at it,* with innermost rooms, breadboxes in the pantry, Lazy Susan turns, brass wall plates, Hawaiian girl jiggly cups, man jokes, miniatures, with hair before we were unhappy, the crimp, the clench *her mouth as if it were my own,* with purple sands collected in the hours, bottles, before we were born, with sky streaked to its thinnest crimson, with wishing pennies caught in the folds, with all we have built that is still our own, the wide white strokes of her bell sleeves swooping

Mother

baby-dolled, daisy-chained, herringboned, terry-clothed, miniskirted, halter-topped, Mary-Kayed, high-waisted, seersuckered, Nivea'd, tube-topped, pinstriped, shoulder-padded, cowl-necked, angel-sleeved, hairsprayed, crocheted, silver-chained

Mother,

I platform you

TRACK 2

backrow badboys Big-League chew your bubblegum jeans as you
hula-hoop hip past the eyes in home ec stirring more than the
cream-puff mix and quick-rise batter, after all these years the last-
dance tension in your thighs, his Stairway to Heaven rabbit-foot
stiffness pressed to your looking-for-luck-in-all-the-*TruthDare
DoubleDarePromisetoRepeat* places,   tongue   tip   testing
frozen metal, a silence peeled and spit, red petals in the snow
all the way home his four o'clock touching behind the old brick
schoolhouse in the brownbag rustle of deadgrass mom will
pick from your hair without questions all this quite naturally a
big part of the problem your heart throbbing a strobe of bass from
Another One Bites the Dust, and all this still without irony as the
Saints' rollerboys in black boot covers approach with one leg
extended and one hand held out not quite all the way choosing her
and her and you, you are telling it like this, you are laying it down
in all that survives the blue tunnel walls, snowpants shushing our
muffled little *helps:* daylight collapses around a thin bead of light,
it was all we needed   just one   star   to save us

SNAKESKIN

*Perhaps at very bottom every horror is something helpless,
that wants help from us.*

>   Rainer Maria Rilke

It is the body lies with its skin—

*Robed in my words I say the snake
changes its skin out of honesty.*

>   Robin Blaser

To the body where our fear meets:

a stria, a stretchmark
cast body of what we were we were.

What I saw slipped its long chains in the grass, a past
linked from tip to cap, tail to milky brille

of eye. It held me in its dark mirror, slim tremble

in the unblinking of woodshed, scale by scale
in the surviving of ghosts, one skin at a time.

When we have loved you enough, body
where our fear parts, will you show us

what we are when we are
unafraid, changing?

I carry it around in a cage.
But a cage can't hold this.

What we want to but won't
crawl through. The bars,

reptilian eyes.

                                          Imagine your body as a tunnel.

                                          Mother, in this you feared me.

                                          In this, you are my ghost.

Teneral roots, bright underhair
clinging. A girl
    slipped through

wire, diamond jags
at her back.

        Somewhere we are becoming
        ourselves—
          where the light dulls
        where my eyes moon anaemic

Mother, you know,
you know the lack a girl finds
behind velvet curtains,
circled in the vile
squirm beneath sheets.

        Oh to give you this, the old
        skin I have come for, the sheen
        still there on its long white
        neck—the swallow—

        If I carry it gently, gently
        will the tremble crawl
        from our arms?

When a girl grows a girl
her need for privacy, internal

resonances. What she can't hear
through the refrigerator hum

she eats. When a girl grows a girl
she is caught looking for something,

an imprint of the inside
of herself. What she finds is

all give, nude nylon
bowed at the knees.

This is how fear becomes tenderness:
in the folding of a field, blade by blade,
in the sidewinding waves
of all we haven't named:

> *somewhere we are twelve years old*
> *and you are losing your father*
> *and I am losing my innocence*

In the pattern of loss:
a stopped heart, a small bleed.

In the curious way it wants you:
next to a circus python's six feet of lack,
in the drowned glow of its pool-tile back.

In the ease with which we draw closer
to the resistance hung on a handler's neck,
the unkilling that beckons a crowd.

> If it is true, Mother, if
> fear is hooked
> on the tempted
>
> then let's move in,
> let's move in and
> stroke the horror.

Fear List:

—dried fruit tough meat pale wads chewed spit flushed napkins large pills choking on ice cubes fish bones

—DIY perms body waves wrinkles cellulite being seen not being seen hair growing out of its settings

—swimming pools change rooms indecision in front of mirrors not having what you have the hips the curve the bra the straps being fat skinny freakishly angled under jeans straying too far from our colour chart *is this a spring blue or a summer blue?*

—bridges speed trains loops double-Ferris-wheel inversions

—waterbed mattresses lake foam skin flakes collecting

—becoming you not becoming you turkey giblets poultry cavities reaching in with a bare hand

—skin pressed to glass expiry dates captivity

—uneven surfaces limbless swimmers forgetting remembering small spaces dark spaces glass eyes hidden cameras held breath being seen by you not being seen by you empty refrigerators cold rooms pickled meat your grief out loud your eyelash streaks

—ending here or there finding out being found

Night windows, when we are faced with ourselves
looking out looking in. *What we love we can't see.*

How close we get will depend upon
our desire for what we fear.

Judgment is planted early.
In a tall house along the rails.

An owl collection stares and stares:
Who at your bedroom window? *Who?*

Mother, it is scared. Its tapered face floats
on a black seed. Fear grows. It sees me as I am:

Let's see how close we can get
before turning. Yes, to those roots.

The ones holding up
the side of a mountain.

A girl on the edge readies herself.
See, she knows you. She's trying

to trust something. She wants you to climb
to that point where you have nothing

                                        but a moving edge.
                                        The world adjusts

                                        stone by stone,
                                        under each step

                                        pebbles grieve
                                        the shifting.

We all have our armours.

The pattern repeats:

link link link.

At the open end of a pipe
my rubber boots tapping.

On a dock sunbathing
with an axe. Oh to let down

our guard:

for the woodpile to hand over its live ones,
for the nameless to show us how safe it really is.

Back lane tar blisters,
the sweet hours
pop.

Now creosote crusts,
haematitic scabs.
The picking never stops.

Of the snake asleep in the brim of my hat,
in the glass of my uncorked dream—

> *Does it matter how lightly*
> *we step over the holes?*

Of the ghost asleep at the tunnel mouth
in the whitespace of a parched tongue—

> *Do we need to name you?*

Of what has come apart alone, tunnelling—
Of what has been poked awake with a long stick—

> *Step back into lesser fields,*
> *we shouldn't be walking here.*

Approach is recorded low,
undulant shadow at our heels.

In being seen we have first to claim
what we cannot crawl from

in ourselves. There is the ghost we are
feeding and underneath—

Maybe some things aren't meant
to be found:

let the field have its lost,
let the lost its never-ending.

What survived us in those hours?
I thought I was in bed with an owl.

An axe on my breath. The hunt.

It was all I could do to look
at what looked back:

a dark gash, slender parting.

Mother, it feels us.
It feels us coming.

A white sheet outlines the body.

Yours or mine?

Story of escape:
fresh snowfall on the pet boa
wound up in a lilac. Infinite story

of the figure 8 frozen on its side.
Mauve petals in the spring

peeling.

I could offer up my fear
but hold it, an owl feather
split in the wind.

And that will be the beauty,
knowing which darknesses
to keep, and which

her her her   *all this*

to give away.

With each breath the minute
avalanche of cells, regeneration.

                              In our listening, words lie down.
                              In our breath, a skin of frost.

Something shivers off
in this tunnel air.

TRACK 3

you were the boy and this is what will keep you *get-your-story-straight-girl* normal, followed all the way home by another boy with a snake down his pants and the just-spit skeleton of a frog, you learn quickly how to pick small bones from your hair, and later on carrots, how not to leave teeth marks, improve upon your choking point, to go for depth, the depth you don't yet have enough ass to fill out your size 26s so you layer four pair of leggings and skip gym not wanting them to see how soft it really is beneath the basement stairs touching in furnace room flicker, girl on girl, we were playing something out the way we all want what is behind glass amber horizons of whiskey bottles marked by your father's lowering expectation a standard maintained by simple dilution, *to water yourself down,* all it takes is a freak show to make you feel less strange, a bearded lady smeared behind monkey-house glass, except the fingerprints were on the outside, the fingerprints were left by us, caught in a house-of-mirrors panic: not knowing the inside   from the out

THE HUMMINGBIRD VIGNETTES

—to be what we thot—transcendent at
a beer table. voice. music. fun. who knows? it's like a sinuous
journey with an edge—a line of light before dark, an opening.

                        Barry McKinnon

THE BIRD

the bird that I freed from the green 7-Up bottle thrown at the girl who told my dad I sang *shake your boobies* instead of *shake your booties*, the bird of relativity shaped to the 2.5 percent of its body that pieces seconds into tens, a nickelweight bird with the largest heart in the animal kingdom, bird of vanishings, beating itself edgeless, tragic

pet bird found limp with its head in the Coke bottle, the caged bird of diary entries, lead bars, crossed-out bird with the pencil-eraser-sized heart, bird of impossible distances, unmapped, shattered on concrete, *you're grounded for the weekend* alone in your bedroom purr of the Conair-dryer-set-on-low bird, the magnifying mirror set on *shadow-free* bird with a three-panel split to light my face at every turn

I make myself up

RUBY-THROATED

Suckneck hickey.

Love arrives
in black spandex,
winebottle swervy.

Hover, the dark peaks
of her, hiphorns

circling. The luster,
a thrust inside her
every

small
revved
wave.

FLAMING SAMBUCA

A spark flares
in our palms,

shot glasses,
sapphire birds.

Take it back
and back,

our dancing bodies
in the dancing light,

the lip-synched licorice
drink. *What'll it be girls?*

A Paralyzer
or a kiss?

Pour us clear
and numb
and burning.

HOVER

Just above
who we are

high enough
to forget

anything
so final

as the dress
on the floor.

WHIRLPOOL

So we slutted a decade.
Or worse, we didn't
and still looked like *that*.

It was not meant to be sad,
our slur of bodies in the hot tub.
Our fevered, beer-buzzed

haze. We wanted to be seen
by the ones who weren't
looking. First, strangers.
Then later, ourselves.

Jet pressures, there and there.
The steam as we rise, a nightgown
slipped. Ghosts, ghosts
on the loose.

FACE CARE

For so long
manoeuvring
myself:

left eye, right,
blur of the made
face, a palette

of shadows.

To avoid
fine-tissue damage
dot the skin
around your eyes
with the ring finger
of your lesser hand.

Make it a habit
to touch yourself
barely.

FIELD TEST

Twenty years measuring
strangers' eyes, entire fields
of vision. Despair and happiness

look the same in the iris:
synaptic blue roots, wired
cross-attachments.

You tell them what they see:
simple horizon, hot-air balloon.
Not what they feel: trapped, anxious.

Come closer. There I am,
a small horn in the corner.
Can you see, I'm no angel?

Blonde-haired, grey-eyed
allelic motes float. We share

the pressure:
you with your trigger,
me with my flinch.

What do you see in this puff of air?
Test me, Mother, I'm disappearing.

HIGH

Raised without
ground, these fine bird bones

fixed on a state
of peaking.

Up and up
I go, losing shadow.

Lovers fall behind,
make their way home.

I'm already
half-gone, keep me

from coming
down.

MIRRORBALL

Beauty wants you
alone
on the dance floor
in pieces.

STROBE

To reduce the effects
of discomfort and disorientation
we recommend that you
gyrate the ray
for no more than 30 seconds.

BLACKOUT

A keyhole

cut
to fit

my tempted
eye.

GLASS-DOMED

Sleeping with strangers
loneliness thin-
blankets my hands,
wonders how far
I am going to go,
to go.

I make the small talk
smaller. *Far* I say and

speed messes with me,
says a tryst on the train
doesn't count:

where there is no fixed point
to claim us, no eye to

unsmear
the stars.

POSE

Blur her.
The adequate space
to forget.
This time with feeling.

Insert: the photo-fake smile.
Five-minute-booth flashes.
The exposures that keep us
haunted.

MORNING AFTER

Focus on disappearances:
A wing. A night. A girl.

Evidence of a body:
Electric blue eyelash stain.
Lip gloss on white duvet.

Morning, a denial
of light

through floral bedsheets.

A muffle
in the pillow.

Feathers, fingernails
raking the dark.

MIRROR

Uncertain which of us is
free, caught,

to what extent this manoeuvre
saves us from

ourselves. At great speeds toward
a flash of final

recognition: *we are that*

impact. If we could sense our own
prismatic snap,

turn a jewel at the dark
window,

let beauty leave
its lonely mark.

COSMETICS

Once you wear mascara you won't be able to stop.
Beauty is addictive.
And feathered eyes work.

Why, look at you now, waiting among flies
on a hot plank
under the feeder.

Look at the male returning
again and again
and with spark!

But the plain light reassembles you
back to all you aren't.

And you are tired,
tired of making things up.

THE GRAVITRON

In which we waited in line to be swept off our feet by the one that takes us standing, up against a wall, at thirty-three revolutions per minute and a dropped out floor.

Reaching a centripetal force that is equivalent to three times the force of gravity or ripping the crotch right out of our parachute pants.

THE EX

Most of it is carnival. Mask. A cheap high.
He dove from a platform with a rubber
rope around his ankles.
He dove for love.

Later, up against a wall, morning of unmystery.

His white Jockey gitch. Braided *tail*.
Breakfast smoke. *Inhale*.
Lisp. *Don't talk*.

My shadow there in the sharp
light, a curve on the wall

graphing the decline. A little rise
now and then. A blip. His

nicotine nails
tracing me

right down
to the fizzle.

OBSERVATION WHEEL

In the blade flash of pinwheel foil
at Ferris wheel height swept upwards
at filmic speeds spliced with a backdrop
of creaking hinge and burnt-out bulb and
some arm crooked in its ritual around-the-
shoulderness, I was delighted
                                      to find
                                                    my face.

PADDLEWHEEL PRINCESS

Through the soft lens of
steamed portholes

our best moves set
to the forward propulsion

of pickups, Long Island
pitchers, the moon spilled

across the floor to the bottom-
of-the-glass

eye that wants you
to be a tourist

with a rose in your hair,
the reason

Ladies' Night is
selling out.

MIDWAY

It's hard to get close enough.
We flit and flit.
Jewel. Shadow.
Vitamin C. Morning-after pill.

Your wing roulette-tickers
in the background.
What have we got
to lose?

SOUTH

Grand Forks, Fargo, any North Dakota town with a Super8
and a Target. To be out of your mind was really to be
out of your body. Feeling it the next day somewhere
south of yourself. In line for the *more more more* that made us feel
less less less, me, being the fun one, rode the 25¢ mechanical
horse. The mothers held back their children, reined in their purse
straps and I, I bucked like a princess.

SMOKE BREAK

A perch
between head and heart, my hand
held out in mid-twenties epiphany.

Rain
one leaf bowed
        to another
passing   passing
the need.

SUNANGEL

In yellow raglan sleeves and
Noxzema xylophone gleam

I mallet out my solo
elbow-bouyant.

Silver lift of the Bonne Bell eye
shimmer, lids in aurora,

lobes drooped in gold
stars. To play the right

note, somewhere, for you
out there in the crowd

with your cube flash twirling and
a girl in your lens

to call your own.

FIREBIRD

Wheels and tires are not the same thing
he tells me, face distorted in the

blue metallic hood. *Oh* I say
and take the ride,

token-blonde my place
upon the bodies piled

rev by rev in muscle-
car chrome. Winged

street lights flap
in the rear-view.

Curfews expire.

ERASERS

With hand veins painted in Max Factor Fair
she is trying to blend in, tone down,
smooth out her flaws in a pat of matte

powder finish. When she raises her
question, her hand disappears
into pink brick, like all the chalks clapped
from the brush, the clouded
answers.

GARBAGE HILL

WARNING: HILL AND
SURROUNDING AREA
MAY BE HAZARDOUS

Where layers helped hide the junk
so close to the surface. Tires bulged
like boys in rugby pants, their stuffed
jawbreaker mouths.

Boob hill with its jagged glass
freckles, beer-bottle nipples. The rusted
unfinished *love* of *OV* caps.

I kept a growing list
of swear words
in my five-year diary:

Boob. Ass. Shit. Crap.

Dirty dirty girl.

CONNECT

The bedroom jewelled
in clock-radio red.
Minutes like Lite-Brite pegs,
poke poke poke.

My lobe studs in garnet
flash in and out,
the countdown to a cherry
hymen streak.

Connect like Braille, touch to touch
as navel lines up with navel, hair
prickle of thigh after the first thorny
thrust.

Connect like smoke
passed lip to lip,
like words swallowed
in molar clicks, bone coupled
to bone.

BUTTERFLY GLASS

The one my dad makes
that I will later give
to my daughter,

with two red cuts
in the wings,
stained rays bleeding

the window.

LAST CALL

Hover, a state of light
hatted in the blue hour.

Throat, a 1970s
velvet sunset.

Come out from your glass
bird-girl,

this one's for you—

TRACK 4

It was as if the higher the boot the longer the leg. I loved your zipper jeans, the gold-toothed smile, your navel to tailbone confidence, your Billy Idol hips. The way you wore your flaws tough, a space between your teeth holding a straw and later a smoke. You knew what fucking was before you knew the word, *breathe* you would say, *breathe*. The sky can be clear like methane in a vodka bottle, the sky can be glassed with rain. *Fake the inhale*, slip a mickey down the back of your pants, exit with a grade five patrol's sense of power. Back-comb your bangs, starch them in Tame and lay it all down at age twelve on a red velvet bed and wait, wait right there for the fuck of your life. The choose-your-own-adventure you can't go back on. White and blue swings that match the white and blue house. Skinny-leg-pump over sheds, trains, the dead circles of grass when the frame lifts from its sockets, the damp shadow, slugs. Dog fights. Roly Polies. No Backstops Allowed. Serve fast and low, stick to the checkbox future in The School Years memory book (there will always be a year, always a school) the place-your-picture-here rectangles, your UHUed headshot (this is the smile, this is how happy). Nurse. *check*. Pilot. *check*. Dancer. *check*. The year Stewardess replaced Model (big decisions) and all this based on a learning I would like to forget: you were smart enough to know you were playing dumb and dumb enough to think this was smart.

MOTH

Fire begins as a secret.

Anne Simpson

down

    star

down

    stairs

in the long-term storage   pilot-light flicker under the shuffleboard mouthing the soft pound of silver weights on felt we were good girls   made of white cakes Easy-Bakes incandescence in cherry chip, rainbow bit, cupcake, confetti, rising to the light under the poncho the gaucho the panty-silk *pupa* a doll pencil-top-pink rubbing the spot the spot inside fuschia bedcovers chenille caterpillars inching the folds inside the folds inside the *mine mine mine* under the bed with flashlights in our mouths flesh lit from the inside under tongue under silence under moths circling the heat the throb the filament spin of our pudic wing flickering

eight thousand shameful ecstasies

fireside

        hair and hair and

        moths combing
        the light

                        metal eyelets spark
                        your copper rivets

                        hips, points of
                        strain

                        the small of your
                        beltchains, flame

lean
in and in

tell me anything

skinnydip

                          the moon
                          everywhere

            drips

            your

                          heat up against a lake
                          one hundred degrees quivering

                          my finger
                                              your fur

you were always that ghost
of the burn you would become

                          leafsinge
                          closer and closer
                          your lips

imago: dusk

        wornjean blue
        on the edge of
        your buckle
        the pocket the slimfit
        the lowrise

                cut

                        in wood
                        on a ledge
                        naming ourselves
                        innocent

lakeview
from your bed
dark, rocking
the tipped

                cup

                                we were
                                here
                                and here

cocoon

    entire bodies
    dissolve   entire dreams

    underleaf,   lanterns
                      unlit   *our hushed lips*

it will take all night
to reassemble

and silence the most mysterious form of affection
inches my
frenulum   *follow*
                the fold

to the moth the mouth the
open flap

because we cannot emerge
the larval tongue

what I don't say

when you spare the wild strawberry my tongue's crush

when the wood rose gathers bud dew in the night

    when I dream

    wet   wet

       wet   wet

    wings

imago

        night window
        your notes
        pinned in stars

wingspan
at my door
corners lifting

            restless
            by the harsh light

    key tap on glass
    an opening

underwing

        on my way down
        the blue stair
        your hidden—

        I pin you like a brooch
        clasped to my quickening

a line crosses us   wingshadow   on the threshold

        night loosens its birds
        Nymph, Black Witch, Darling, Wife

        come to me
        Inconsolable, Dejected, Sweetheart
        come to me burning

imago

canoeing
a wine bottle rolls empty
fireworks above, a caterpillar of ash
don't let it be over

                                            oil lamp
                                            gasp peak
                                            the room flaps

                                            snap snap

                                            one by one
                                            the buttons up
                                            your back

if I'm making this up

        the paper edge
        is still folded
        by your
        finger

        slipped under, into

        how much do you want this?

dance

        around and around
        the fire, a crinoline spin
        of conifers, underlit

the wild moves in   *every shadow laced*
as I have always wanted   *to your hips, circling*

        fingernails, fireflies
        flirt with the dark

why not

                    now, here, by a small candle?

                    pick me up at the finger
                    carry me to the glass

                    I don't want to be pinned
                    pin me

airless

        curtains sucked
        to their screens

        even the dead pick up on a breath
        in a glass under the lamp, stirring

        there's no hiding

        a body crawled into its own weight
        a moth folded, as if petted there

        wait   the cling can help you
                    understand the fold

where will this end?

with those behind glass
wings, lashes unblinking

with those in the flame
now blow

with a night extinguished
in my palm *talcum, ash*

a dawn
of sparrows

as I reach down, down
into the sorrow

TRACK 5

you hold close to your privacies: morning hair, nakedness, so that
the worry of sleepovers becomes how not to disrupt a curling-ironed
bang, teenage alterations so fierce *layered clothes, painted skin, teased stiff
hair* that you can never let go of your coverings completely, because
you want to be empty and full all at once you try the fudge brownie
visualization, in awe of Charlene Prickett's milky one-litre thighs,
freedom is to walk without sucking in your gut to let go of the never-
let-it-go theories, *pedalling pedalling, banana-seat-streamlined all is safe, all
is sound,* in Princess Di's city-block garden of trailing lace, plastic hair
bands that leave two indents behind your ears and a mildly throbbing
ache that remind you of the small and steady sacrifices you will endure
for beauty—   the truth shall be known in the sheerest nylon,
metal foot measure, the gaps in your red jelly shoes, each flop you take
with rubber lifts glued to your soles to correct *that crooked walk* you
keep them tucked, on the inside, the secrets, like how you invented
a man who lived in the sewer and left Smurfs and Shrinky Dinks
dangling from strings, how the mothers didn't question happy endings
or your gobstoppered windpipe, the pale orb popped from your throat,
arcing—   here's to a world that wants you to crave your own
emptiness, choke on your own fear, a hard butterscotch where your
scream used to be *there are hundreds of tiny bones at the back of your neck*,
she warns, *be careful how high you look up*

LEAF

one small leaf is a heart:
a leaf we divide, dividing us.

John Thompson

I.

Tea Reading

Divine me Mother. I'm trembling. Trace your thirst to my youngest tongue. Your tilt to my emptying. I am here at the bottom of the cup in the distant future. Smiling. I am your negative space, your brightest cut. In the hollies, your spiny red crown. Read your way to me, in your hungers, in and down.

Cordate

Leaves, leaves under skin, private foliages. Dendritic lace. Tiny knots taking. Seed. The ones that decide us. A palm to the chest. Our thinnest heat. Umbra flutter, bedsheets, our tidy fluttering nest. When it is time, promise to meet me here. Under every inconsolable tremble.

Decidua

Even if you have walked freely to this ledge. Even if you have said *yes*. No star will have you in this state. Not even the lowest shivering on blades. It's too late. The earth has cut you from its weight. Now you have to find your way back.

Seed

A twitch

in the heights
of your innermost
gust, a tug

body-stalk primitive.

Streak of longitudes
in the petals
of peeled eyes.

The wind will decide
who you will and will not be.

Linea

Shadow of unexplained longitudes.

Descent

Mother, there were stems thick as wrists,
leaves curled like hands and petals that pried.

There were places in the branches that wept.
I walked with my arms out and tried.

On the carpet tonight something twitched.
I put the chairs together and slept on my knees.

Auriculate

Your voice inside
each viscid ear.

Umbilicus

The leaves are barely alive
still moist at the scar.
Shadow becomes body
where the annelids have dried.

The fall collects our edges,
a furred fecund air.
In the curb-gather, a heave,
feather-chested, crawling.

Somewhere we know
what it is to become
an open wound dragging
one shimmering line.

Lightning

in roots, where the greater faults share us

in heart, where the small skulls flash

in thirst, where the gold milk threads us

in veins, where the storm ripens cloud

in night, where the forked tongues dowse us

Mother, spare me, spare these slender bones

II.

Teardrop
A silver tiara
lowers you
doll-legged
from a cloud.

Hitched
Confetti punctate.
Just Married filigree.
Tin cans clanging

the wide swing of chrome.
O pompoms, honeycomb
bells, carry us home.

Bouquet
At the centre
the grip.

A yellow rose
undercover.

At the cusp
of your new satin

swell, all you
were, will be

tossed up. Stems
raise their sharp

prolonged points.
From one stung hand

to another.

Wedding Cake

No one knows what is inside
the seamless shellac.
On tiers of glass stems,
white rosettes, foil leaves.

At the Kodak moment
we don't imagine emptiness:
a hollow, plastered gasp,
a white sponge to sop up

what we haven't yet faced:
any slab this alive, underknife
quivering.

The blade is not really there
to cut, only to test
a moment in the lens
when hand upon hand
you don't know what
you are dividing.

Flower Girl

More fetal than petal more toes than rose more float than sprout more belief than leaf more *she loves me* than *not* more conceal than real.

Waistlines

i.

Fancy the optics of the tapered gown.
Light through a window shaped like a seed.

The blues were complete with gloves and eyeshadow.
The shoes were complete with a clutch.

How to be that substance you changed your life for:
the centre, the breech in the centre.

Under your skirt, the growing
shadow, the neatly made bed.

You and your mother in the tulip mirror.
Her shadow, your veil.

When nothing is between.
Everything is between.

The gold band
and the kiss.

ii.

Where I am afraid to be more than you.
All I want is to be more than you.

To collapse in the middle.
Asleep with a twitch.

To root and root the luminous
starches of the heart.

Through walls.
Through living walls.

Let out
our seams.

NOTES

The introductory epigraph by Robert Kroetsch is from "Statements by the Poets" in *The Long Poem Anthology*.

The second epigraph is from Lyn Hejinian's *My Life*. The line *"what education serves us if at all"* in "TRACK 1" is also from *My Life*, and *"it it it it"* was written prior to discovering Robin Blaser's poem of the same title in *Moth Poem*.

NEST: The epigraph is from Carolyn Forché's "On Earth" in *Blue Hour*.

SNAKESKIN: The epigraphs are from Rainer Maria Rilke's *Letters to a Young Poet* (translated by K. W. Maurer) and Robin Blaser's "Herons" in *The Holy Forest*.

THE HUMMINGBIRD VIGNETTES: The epigraph is from Barry McKinnon's "Arrythmia" as it appears in *The New Long Poem Anthology*.

MOTH: The epigraph is from Anne Simpson's *Quick*. "Down star" refers to the Latin origin of "desire" as derived from the verb *desiderare*: *de*, "down"; *sider*, "star." Carolyn Forché's lines *"and silence the most mysterious form of affection"* and *"because we cannot emerge"* are from "On Earth" in *Blue Hour*. "Pudic" refers to the pudendal nerve, a wing-shaped spread of eight thousand nerve endings in the clitoral glans, and derives from the Latin *pudere*, "be ashamed."

LEAF: The epigraph is from John Thompson's "ghazal XXIV" in *Stilt Jack*. "Decidua" is the uterine lining during pregnancy that is shed with the placenta. "Linea" refers to the *linea nigra*, a dark vertical line that appears between the navel and the pubis during pregnancy.

Chalk drawings, anonymous, Oak Street sidewalk, Winnipeg.

TRACK 2 and SNAKESKIN are for Kev.

ACKNOWLEDGEMENTS

To the Saskatchewan writing community and the Saskatchewan Arts Board and The Canada Council for the Arts for supporting the creation of this work.

To the editors of *Grain*, *Matrix*, *CV2* and *boulderpavement* for publishing earlier versions of some of these poems and to JackPine Press for the chapbook *Nest*.

To the McLachlans (Saskatoon), George and Jean Lidster (Torch River) and Ethel and Ken Wills (Eastend) for spaces that hold both writing and family.

To the Girdwood girls, then and now: Chrissy, Jen, Heather, Kerry, Jinx and Shell.

To Jennifer Beaudry for handmade marvels and Ariel Gordon for wooly Winnipeg camaraderie.

For Saskatchewan connections with no bounds: Holly Luhning, Jeanette Lynes, The JackPines, The Crackt poets, The Molnars, Olivia Newhouse, Erin Bidlake, Emma Williams, Tamara Bond, Amalie Atkins, Betsy Rosenwald, Nancy Tam and all who make it home.

Sylvia Legris for midnight train-song serenades.

Monique Blom for nothing less than wonder.

The 2008 Sage Hill night owls: dee hobsbawn-smith and Michael Bradford.

Barry Dempster, Kitty Lewis, Alayna Munce, Cheryl Dipede and Alan Siu for the glorious Brick process and experience. With special thanks to Alayna for punctuating it all with such care.

To Daphne Marlatt for tapping gently.

To Sandra Ridley for a friendship carved in wood.

To Liz Philips, sagacious editor, for deep-in-the-woods transformations and the x-axis to nail it!

To Dad for holding the lens, Grandma for the cookies, Kev for early-morning cable, Claire for sisterhood and Jack for the long walks through everything.

As ever, to Abby and Ben, my levity, my ground. Darren, partner in solitude.

And Mom, for answering without fail, long calls home from the threshold.

Jennifer's first collection of poems, *Saltations* (Thistledown Press, 2005) was nominated for three Saskatchewan Book Awards. An earlier version of Girlwood won the 2008 John V. Hicks Manuscript Award and a Saskatchewan Emerging Artist Award.

"The Hummingbird Vignettes" and "Moth" were finalists in the 2008 CBC Literary Awards and "Nest" appeared as a limited-edition chapbook with JackPine Press in fall 2010.

After many sunny years in Saskatoon, Jennifer now lives in Winnipeg in a tall yellow house with her husband and two children.